T0282239

Auras AND chakras

THE INCREDIBLE CONNECTION BETWEEN THE SUBTLE BODIES AND THE ENERGY OF THE UNIVERSE

Publisher
Balthazar Pagani

Editorial coordination
Elena Cattaneo

Graphic design
Bebung

Vivida

Vivida® is a registered trademark property of White Star s.r.l.
www.vividabooks.com

© 2023 White Star s.r.l.
Piazzale Luigi Cadorna,6
20123 Milano, Italia
www.whitestar.it

Translation: TperTradurre s.r.l., Rome
Editing: Phillip Gaskill

ISBN 978-88-544-2037-3
2 3 4 5 6   28 27 26 25 24

Printed in China

The contents of this book are the result of research and studies conducted by the author
over more than twenty years, and which he shares during his workshops and seminars.
However, upon the onset or persistence of ailments and symptoms you should consult a
doctor for an accurate diagnosis.

LUCA APICELLA

Auras AND chakras

**THE INCREDIBLE CONNECTION BETWEEN THE SUBTLE
BODIES AND THE ENERGY OF THE UNIVERSE**

ILLUSTRATIONS BY
**Alessandra
De Cristofaro**

Vivida

contents

FOREWORD

Introducing people to the aura that surrounds living beings means immerging them in a world that is invisible to most, but instead reveals all of the beauty and pure, unconditional love of the cosmos.

Learning that energies are absorbed from the environment around us through energy centers, **chakras**, is a surprising experience, and it is even more surprising to understand how these energies are channeled to the centers of belonging by means of the **meridians**.

Nature is always able to find her own balance, but human beings sometimes forget that they are an integral part of this nature, continuing to ignore how the constant violations they perpetuate on her they are also inflicting upon themselves.

> INTRODUCTION <

Living on Earth, the planet of great emotions and beauty, is a huge honor that within the whole solar system is granted to just 8 billion people, but in order to live a full, satisfying life it is important that our existence is in perfect harmony.

This volume offers some techniques and advice useful in the search for balance even after having gone through difficult, tempestuous times. It is in fact important to identify and correct your dysfunctional habits in order to try and implement—even through the smallest of decisions—a significant improvement in your life span.

You have to know yourself, and you have to discover your own subtle functioning to understand that there is always a precise logic in life and that events are rarely random.

THE MULTILEVEL STRUCTURE

A Glance Beyond the Human

In the most critical moments of life what unites human beings—be they religious or atheist, disciples of philosophies or New Age followers— is the search for something that is present beyond the earthly permanence.

Taking a glance upwards, even in a bad mood, or retreating to a secluded place to isolate yourself, is an implicit request for help.

When difficult moments arise in life, such as illness or accident, many people resort to what some religions refer to as "the fear of God": the fear of having done something wrong in the eyes of their own god or deity.

This means it is vital to understand what happens beyond (or rather perhaps around) the heads of human beings and start to take our first steps in a land that is unknown to the many and only really understood by serious scholars of esotericism.

God and Humans

The word "religion" comes from the Latin *religio*, from the verb *religare* (bind), thus signifying the principle of a connection with something superhuman.

In the Christian religion, for example, supernatural truth is revealed to all through the institution of the Church and its representatives in order to be universally accepted. Other religions also have a mediator through whom to pass. What would happen if, on the other hand, we tried to do without the mediator and simply actively listened to the divine part ourselves?

The Divine Pyramid Structure

It is important we try not to imagine divinity—in its own multitude of meaning—as a supreme being who intervenes to punish humans when they make mistakes.

Instead, we should try to consider this superior entity—God as he is known by convention—as a complex organized system, a pyramidal hierarchical structure.

This structure can be conceived as an organization in perpetual activity operating on several levels, with its employees at the base (i.e., the workers) and the boss in charge of everything and everyone, the organizing mind that puts its own ideas into work.

It is an intercommunicating structure based on hierarchies in which the part closest to the human being, made up of guides and angels, act as the first channel of communication also based on the type of sensitivity that humankind manifests with the divine part. A pathology, for example, conveys a message. If it is understood, the subject will most likely stop the dysfunction or, at the least, not allow it to repeat.

So, it is important to understand that the higher entity we call God is actually a complex organized system.

THE PHYSICAL BODY AND THE ENERGIC BODY

In the West, over the past two hundred years, society has been driven by the idea that seeing is believing. The assertion is that everything that is not scientifically explainable is not real. I personally think that over time, through sensitivity and knowledge, this belief will reverse.

Investigating beyond the senses of the physical body has allowed me to make some interesting discoveries: for example, that the functioning of organs such as the brain remain largely misunderstood. Only one thing seems to be certain: everything depends on it.

This organ is subordinated to an etheric apparatus which sends it messages to be carried out: the aura and its layers send the two hemispheres information to be carried out without delay. A physical function, a pathology or healing occurs through these orders that come "from above" so that an evolutionary path can be undertaken.

To say that the physical and energetic bodies are separate is incorrect, it would be like saying that the spirit is found only in heaven and matter only on earth, and that each one does its own thing. What happens is, in fact, the exact opposite. If it is true that the body uses energy obtained through the absorption of foods, it is equally true that it uses an etheric fuel so that the energy system governing the body can work.

In the search for spirituality, therefore, we must place our attention back to the very point at which we find the beginning of everything, the union of matter with the subtle, or rather, the heart.

LIVING BEINGS AND PLANET EARTH

Within the solar system, the Earth is known as the Blue Planet. On the subtle level, it is a planet with a high emotional impact, where the water that covers it in such a large percentage is the archetype.

Compared to the other planets and stars in the solar system, living on Earth allows us to enter more quickly into contact with a high number of emotions that can make us evolve.

Imagining the Earth as a static celestial body, made up of simple dense matter, is wrong since *Gaia*, similarly to the human energy system, consists of a dense electromagnetic network, with an auric field that makes it alive and in constant evolution. The planet has a series of energy centers, or chakras, with a flow of energy that goes in and out—just as if it were breathing. Just think, for example, of sea and air currents that can be used in the exchange of energy and information.

The living beings that inhabit the Earth live in an articulated context, as if they were immersed in a subtle soup of energies, also known as the information field, which keeps them in close connection with each other. This union is possible through the auric bodies found in differing amounts and conformations in all mineral, vegetable, animal, and human beings which are constantly exchanging information and knowing each other before they meet in the physical sense.

Hermes Trismegistus reaffirms the concept that things are the same both in the dense and subtle parts of the Earth and that the only way to find balance is through the union of the two parts that can never be separated. "That which is above is like to that which is below, and that which is below is like to that which is above to perform the miracle of the unique thing" (*Emerald Tablet*).

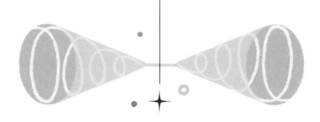

the CHAKRAS

The chakras work in a complex system of energies. This ingenious machine is powered by the flow of subtle energies, in which every single cell functions thanks to fuel. If we think of the circulatory system, we know with scientific certainty that blood constantly needs an engine, the heart, to nourish the tissues. To that we add the vasoconstriction and vasodilatation of the veins and arteries, which guarantee a widespread, homogeneous flow throughout the body. The same can be said of the etheric fuel that nourishes the body and which uses the approximately 44,000 chakras that distribute the energies in a balanced way as a motor.

Where there is no blood there is necrosis and therefore death, just like the absence of etheric energy in the body.

The chakra system includes a series of conical structures, positioned in pairs on the narrowest base, which, rotating in the opposite direction, generate a sort of suction of energy. When the energy

runs out from the functions, it is expelled outwards by the chakras themselves. It is an energetic respiration that never stops, just like the respiratory system.

It is important to know that the seven known chakras are those found within the human body which perform the more important energy work. Their functions can be considered equal to those performed by the heart.

Then there are the so-called etheric chakras, which are found outside the physical body and located on the subtle bodies, where they perform the important task of connecting the external environment with the internal one of the human body. The so-called physical chakras receive energy from the outside through some etheric chakras found on the aura. These make up the etheric energy in six colors which are then channeled towards the respective chakras that will release said energy. Therefore, red towards the first chakra, orange towards the second, yellow towards the third and so on.

Physical Chakras

T he ancient Indian Vedic texts, an integral part of the Hindu religious teachings, detail the chakras. In particular, they identify seven as engines with greater lift than the over forty thousand remaining chakras present in the physical and subtle bodies. These are in fact the centers through which the greatest energy absorption passes which will then be spread to all the others. Getting to know them helps a deep understanding of how human beings work (and others too) and the actions to be taken in case of problems that concern them.

FIRST CHAKRA
Muladhara

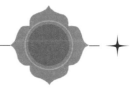

Message from Muladhara

I deal with the genital area, through which man exists and from which he comes. Humans can lose themselves here in the urges of food, sex, money. Heinous crimes can be committed to possess material things, but the world asks to evolve from the earth, from the dark and black color from which we find ourselves and from the red in which we boil. We will have to learn in a balanced way to take and —through the primal movement of the final part of the intestine, to give and to give yourself to the world.

Physical location
Genital area; perineal area, between the vagina or testicles and the anus.

Natural element
Earth.

Number of lotus petals in Indian iconography
4.

Numerology
Number 4: manifestation on Earth.

Associated color
Red with the power to activate energy, the fire of foundation; black with the power to ground you to the Earth.

Action
To exist through one's body.

Managed emotions
Fear; pleasure; physical well-being; survival.

Governed glands
Ovaries and testicles: transformation and creation.

Organs
Vagina; testicles; penis; skeletal system; muscular system; nails; teeth.

Emotional function
Right to be on Earth and therefore to exist; grounding to the Earth; resilience; aggression; generosity.

Mental function
Daily practicality through the rationalization of things.

Spiritual function
Evolution through the experimentation of the material.

Malfunctions
The first chakra essentially governs a type of energy that oversees the dense part of the body in its most basic functions. It is linked to the management of money and sexuality and all forms that lead a human being towards a balanced existence through the material world.

Rebalancing practices
Contact with nature, for example Forest Therapy; walking barefoot; rooting exercises; African dances; active meditation.

SECOND CHAKRA
Swadhisthana

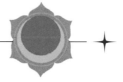

Message from Swadhisthana

The body fluids that I administer symbolize the feminine side of each of us and the emotions that I deal with. Emotions are wonderful, but —if managed incorrectly—they can cause considerable discomfort and pathologies. These are to be interpreted as a message which, if understood, can heal entire areas of human life.

Physical location
About 1.5 in below the navel.

Natural element
Water.

Number of lotus petals in Indian iconography
6.

Numerology
Number 6: what is created.

Associated color
Orange.

Action
Feeling emotion.

Managed emotions
All of them.

Governed glands
Adrenal glands: fight or flight.

Organs
Uterus; ovaries; prostate; bladder; intestine; kidneys.

Emotional function
Feel personal emotions, process them, and let go of what you don't need.

Mental function
Balance the mind with emotions.

Spiritual function
Getting to know each other through emotions and understand yourself, evolving.

Malfunctions
Some consider drowning in your emotions unseemly as it indicates dishonor to oneself or to others. The second chakra deals in fact, with honor, together with the development of one's own personal power which, if balanced, will allow you manage emotionally-charged moments and situations. The second chakra—through the first—works to find practical and emotional means to survive the emergency, until you can integrate the experience as constructive and valuable.

Rebalancing practices ....
Self-listening techniques; meditation and movement with water; theater; expressive techniques.

THIRD CHAKRA
Manipura

Message from Manipura

Human beings can achieve much through their ego. Through the egoic structure man protects his own fragilities and, only when these have been healed, can the ego be put to the service of others to build and not crush.

Physical location
Close to the mouth of the stomach, between the navel and the sternum.

Natural element
Fire.

Number of lotus petals in Indian iconography
10.

Numerology
Number 10 - the beginning and the end of everything, fulfillment.

Associated color
Golden yellow.

Action
Manifestation of power acquired internally in the second chakra, and which now reflects outwards.

Managed emotions
Anxiety, vitality: I am.

Governed glands
Pancreas: managing the sweet, affectionate part of life.

Organs
Stomach; spleen; pancreas; liver; gallbladder; small intestine; diaphragm.

Emotional function
I exist by performing actions; I make real what I feel inside, establishing myself in the world.

Mental function
Everyone sees me, therefore I know I exist.

Spiritual function
Putting my power to the service of my personal evolution and that of the world.

Malfunctions
The worst tyrant is he who has not yet learned to draw sustenance from himself for his own needs. As he is unable to, he believes that the only way to get nourishment is through others, taking what he needs through any means possible, even the most despotic or childish. Others are no longer seen as worthy of love or respect; he only thinks of his own needs to be satisfied at all costs. The tantrum of a child is often the same as that of a tyrant.

Rebalancing practices
Individual sports and activities; volunteering; light a fire to warm yourself and then invite others to share it with you; practice of unconditional love.

FOURTH CHAKRA
Anahata

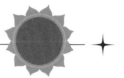

Message from Anahata

Giving without asking for anything in return. Transforming all heavy emotions into light and clean energy. Bringing information throughout the energy circuit. Connecting with human and superhuman love. I bear pain in critical moments and refine emotions. This is my job.

Physical location
In the center of the chest.

Natural element
Air.

Number of lotus petals in Indian iconography
12.

Numerology
Number 12: overcoming and transformation.

Associated color
Green, like emeralds, and thick, like the color of malachite in emotional processing; pink in support.

Action
Transformation of heavy energy to light; emotional support; strong ability to diffuse high frequencies throughout the body and around it.

Managed emotions
Love.

Governed glands
Thymus gland: personal discernment between good and evil.

Organs
Heart; lungs; thymus gland; circulatory system.

Emotional function
Pain release through dissolution.

Mental function
Autonomy: loving in a deep, unconditional way, without asking for anything in return.

Spiritual function
Connecting the heart to energies of the cosmos, opening oneself to the service of the world, for example through Reiki.

Malfunctions
The fourth chakra tells how an excessively tender heart may lead to giving oneself and loving too much, until we lose sight of ourselves.
At the same time, when the chakra is blocked, a bitter heart can harden to such an extent as to let nothing in again.

Rebalancing practices
Volunteering; looking after others; acts of unconditional love and humility in which one learns to receive unreservedly from others; gardening; listening to Gregorian chants; a healthy lifestyle.

FIFTH CHAKRA
Vishudda

Message from Vishudda

The willpower to act in the world belongs to me. I can help you materialize your will through verbalization. Communication and swallowing are my tasks, and I use the thyroid gland to push human beings to evolve.

Physical location
At the base of the neck.

Natural element
Ether.

Number of lotus petals in Indian iconography
16.

Numerology
Number 16: Liberation from all mental, physical, and relational conditioning, which can only happen through a spontaneous process of total opening up towards the world.

Associated color
Blue.

Action
Power to act; internal and external communication.

Managed emotions
Courage.

Governed glands
Thyroid, the gland of human evolution.

Organs
Throat and thyroid.

Emotional function
Telling the world who you are and materialization.

Mental function
Ability to flow, following what you are deep down.

Spiritual function
What is communicated becomes the truth; experiencing new boundaries and overcoming them.

Malfunctions
By searching for what you want intensely, we learn to materialize it after having verbalized it. The thyroid, in its butterfly shape, demands evolution, going beyond one's limitations and finding new boundaries to experience and overcome.

Rebalancing practices
Artistic practices such as writing and reading to broaden one's own awareness; singing and sacred music; rebirthing as a means of exceeding limits.

SIXTH CHAKRA
Ajna

Message from Ajna

Only those who ask themselves questions and have a thirst for truth and decided to see, will be given the ability to see things as they truly are. The first look is aimed within ourselves, to seek the truth that is often found in the unexplored shadows. The next step is the vision of the supersensitive reality in which human beings have always been immersed, but that few decide to explore.

Physical location
Between the eyebrows.

Natural element
Light.

Number of lotus petals in Indian iconography
2.

Numerology
Number 2: the descent of the breath of spirit in matter.

Associated color
Indigo.

Action
Vision.

Managed emotions
Trust of the new and hope in the future.

Governed glands
Pituitary: the command center of everything.

Organs
Respiratory and visual system (eyes, ears, nose, paranasal sinus); cerebellum; nervous system; hormone system.

Emotional function
Courage: be willing to see the truth, come what may.

Mental function
Lucidity: truth will make people understand and then comprehend things.

Spiritual function
Supersensitive laws are the same as the terrestrial ones; "As above, so below" (Hermes Trismegistus).

Malfunctions
In the world of information that immerses mankind so, truth and lies exist alongside each other. By deciding to see the truth, we cannot avoid the bitter truth that some beliefs—some perhaps that were at the very basis of our certainties—are false.

Rebalancing practices

Meditation; zazen meditation; development exercises with quartz balls; bibliotherapy, i.e., reading to get to know oneself and others; try your hand in experiences to introduce us to new worlds; psychotherapeutic or holistic activities to identify and manage one's own part in shadow.

SEVENTH CHAKRA

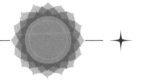

Sahasrara

Message from Sahasrara

The most advanced technologies can only offer us a fraction of what can be obtained from the cosmos by connecting through me. And it is exactly in that moment, following a trauma or an erratic lifestyle, when you unconsciously decide to disconnect that you become an automaton, untethered from yourself and from what you are deep down.

Physical location
At the top, in the center of the head.

Natural element
Ether.

Number of lotus petals in Indian iconography
1000.

Numerology
Number 1000, or 1: the beginning of everything.

Associated color
Indigo.

Action
Connection.

Managed emotions
Human emotions connect with the divine and learns to integrate it.

Governed glands
Epiphysis: human impressions are connected to divine ones, lending the fruits of new knowledge to the human part.

Organs
Brain.

Emotional function
Lack of emotion due to the connection to the divine matrix of superhuman nature.

Mental function
Understanding beyond the mind: insight.

Spiritual function
Knowing why you exist.

Malfunctions
A disconnect or erroneous connection through the seventh chakra leads to problems in nourishment, on various levels: physical, emotional, psychological, and spiritual. For example, on a physical level this could be anorexia, which is reflected in a lack of nourishment throughout all of the above-mentioned parts. When we are not properly aligned with the seventh chakra, we risk swapping health nourishment for other types of elements that are often harmful. Unalignment becomes a possible way of escaping the hardships we come against every day while managing our emotions.

Rebalancing practices ···
Meditation; grounding practices that succeed the meditative ones.

Etheric Chakras

Here is yet another piece of the wonderful divine machine, in which we have been able to observe how the physical and subtle bodies work inextricably together. The chakras are responsible for providing the body with fuel to ensure a fine, accurate function.

So beyond the physical body are the etheric chakras, which perform functions that are much less palpable yet essential to connect humans to the past, present, and whatever the future will bring.

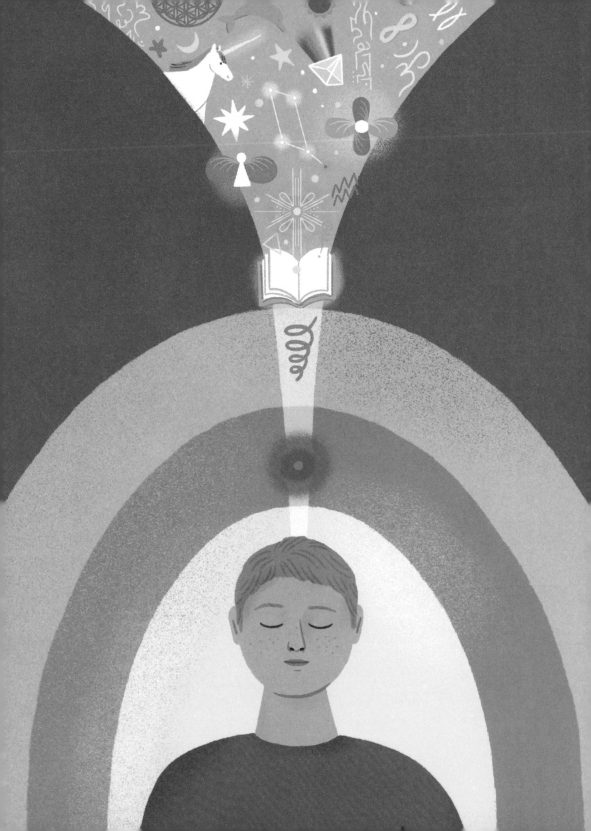

SOUL STAR CHAKRA

The Soul Star is located just above the crown chakra (the last of the seven chakras located at the top of the head) and its colors are emerald green and purple.

It is the center that connects the physical body to the energic body, allowing subtle energies to enter the physical body through the procurement of the seven chakras.

It is the chakra that comes into contact with dimensions beyond the earthly, allowing you to remember past lives through flashes of images or situations. It is therefore important to understand how it is relevant to connect your present consciousness with memories of the past.

Indeed, such connections allow us to lift the veil of previous lives so that you can remember and recognize places and people who may help us, in our present incarnation, take those steps that in the past were left incomplete or incorrect.

The Soul Star is the energic center that permits interaction with the celestial front line, that of the guides and angels.

ALTA MAJOR CHAKRA

The cerebellum chakra, or rather the intuitive chakra, is located at the back, at the base of the neck and its color is emerald green. It is called the "fourth eye" for its high perceptive capacity: it protects the person and acquires information to be transferred within the energy system for re-elaboration, allowing a better and deeper physical-energetical perception of the surrounding environment.

Here we find the atlas, the first cervical vertebra, which deals with ensuring the flow of channeled energy from the top of the head to within the energy system of the physical body. When the atlas vertebra is unaligned, limited energy can pass, thereby reducing the function of the energy system.

Insight, genius, they all come from here.
The Alta Major chakra works
on creativity, it helps to see events
from a different point of view,
intuitively understanding
the real dynamics of them.

CENTRAL STAR CHAKRA

The Central Star chakra is located near the diaphragm and is golden in color.

The soul, made up of an intangible substance, chooses the dense body to express itself. The Central Star chakra therefore becomes the fulcrum of research for the direction of the soul as it evolves through experimentation of the physical body and by means of the senses; it becomes the point of the energy circuit at which the etheric chakras meet—the bridge between the Soul Star chakra and the earth chakra.

This chakra is responsible for the expansion and strengthening of the self, favoring the activation of energies that allow you to connect to the whole in a harmonic way. Through the Central Star chakra, you are gifted the gifts of knowledge to cultivate and grow, developing them, and evolving through them.

Righteousness in the Service of the Cosmos comes from this chakra, which asks us to march through life without compromise, learning to be small as an insect yet authoritative as titans, but always in love and with a helpful ego.

EARTH STAR CHAKRA

The Earth Star chakra is positioned about one feet below the feet and is red and green in color. It works to convey the energies from the Earth, helping us to connect to it.

It leads us to a harmonious life, but when imbalanced it causes great existential difficulties in us, and we end up searching for a different dimension to the earthly one, towards the house of spiritual origin.

The Earth Star allows us to rise towards a vision of life that passes through a deep rooting, in which the more connected we are with Mother Earth, the more our bond with the flora and fauna. It is like becoming a tree evolving skywards, towards the spiritual part, experiencing the frequencies of the Earth.

It is well known that shamans are very familiar with the connection between their relationship with the Earth and the healing influences which ensue.

MERIDIANS

It is, therefore, clear that energies are being pushed into the body by the system of approximately 44,000 chakras.

Their flow is channeled through the pathways that touch the physical and subtle body in its entirety. The meridians, made up of non-palpable structures, are studied in traditional Chinese medicine and become pathways along which we can find some of the remaining chakras that have not yet been mentioned here. Smaller in size, they work to push the energies—the *ki*—along the meridians—also known as *nadi* ("channel" in Sanskrit)—which then nourish the whole body at the cellular level.

There are twelve main meridians divided into pairs: each one is associated with one of the five elements of traditional Chinese medicine found in nature: water, wood, earth, metal, and fire (the latter is an exception as it is linked to two pairs, so four meridians). As well as these elements which mark the beginning and end of the cycle of life,

meridians are also associated with the seasons in which each pair finds the most important expression of its function. This also helps us recognize the emotions linked to each meridian.

It is also important to learn about the biological clock of the meridians, i.e., the time slots in which they release the most energy. Depending on the ease or difficulty with which energy flows through or is hoarded by the organs, ease or unease is created in the body itself. If, for example, you wake at approximately the same time each night, it is a good idea to look into the cause as it is a warning light of emotional and physical events, or rather a window to the functioning of the organs and meridians. For example, if you wake between 3:00 a.m. and 5:00 a.m., this indicates the lung meridian.

Knowing the system and functioning of the meridians allows you to interpret seemingly insignificant daily events and understand more clearly some symptoms or illnesses at the physical, emotional, psychological, and spiritual level.

KIDNEY MERIDIAN

Twin meridian
Bladder.

Season
Winter.

Element
Water.

Solar time
5-7pm.

Predominant emotion
Fear.

Feature
Point where the creator energy lies, the origin of humankind. The Kidney Meridian deals with transforming energy provided by food into nourishment, blending it with the etheric.

Strengths
It is the seat of will which, if balanced, allows you to accomplish great things in life. It manages the libido. Fear is a base emotion that is often limited to being a negative view of life. It is, however, important to imagine how this comes into our daily lives in a healthy way, helping us see how possibly the situation we are living, or a person or object, may be dangerous for our psychophysical and spiritual integrity. Seen thus, fear is no longer a state of emotion to be avoided or ignored. Quite the opposite: fear is a healthy alarm bell that helps us understand that if we continue along a certain path we may come to harm and invites us to implement caution or simply move towards a different solution.

Weaknesses
On the other hand, the inability to manage fear when it is no longer useful but becomes an obstacle to a healthy personal and social life is a different matter. If *ki*, life energy, runs out, it means the death of the being. It is therefore important to control your quality of life and stress levels—a determining factor in energy (*ki*) running out in your kidneys. In the event of disharmonious energies, it could lead to sexual impotence.

BLADDER MERIDIAN

Twin meridian
Kidney.

Season
Winter.

Element
Water.

Solar time
3-5pm.

Predominant emotion
Fear.

Feature
Essential energy and all those that arise from the subconscious, but which are a fundamental part of themselves. Together with fear—managed profoundly by the kidney meridian—, in particular the bladder rules all those deeply-archived events, memories that should not be left to stagnate but rather let go, just like urine, full of waste materials no longer of use to the body, is. In a balanced condition, all of this is attributed —together with the rigor we use upon ourselves and the world— to the ability to make decisions which, after listening deeply to ourselves, we can decide what is to be kept and what, on the other hand, it is necessary on the physical, emotional, psychological, and spiritual levels must be released.

Strengths
The will to live, to let life flow in all its aspects that, just like water, will be almost impossible to trap. You can't block energy, but you can transform it, keeping it flow.

Weaknesses
Not pursuing our own goals because we are overwhelmed by worry that we don't have enough life energy. Negative memory, which induces us to give up and then transforms into resentment and then hate, can poison our entire existence. Here, we are able to recover energy to get through those difficult moments of life; here is where our longevity depends.

LIVER MERIDIAN

Twin meridian
Gallbladder.

Season
Spring.

Element
Wood.

Solar time
1-3am.

Predominant emotion
Anger.

Feature
The liver meridian is the general, and therefore the strategist of the entire system. Along with the gallbladder, it shows us how action and movement enter our structure without delay; therefore, the energy is sudden and fast. Great willpower is an integral part of the liver meridian.

Strengths
Planning. To transform toxins that would otherwise be harmful to humans into general productive energy.

Determination and control are the characteristics that most stand out. The principle of connection to our personal concept of the divine and "religion."

Weaknesses
If left unchecked, anger is a very harmful emotion. If it explodes roughly, it can cause great damage in the environment. If left unexpressed, anger turns to rage, thereby damaging the body's internal organs and provoking, over time, an energy imbalance that can lead to symptoms and illnesses. This means that the liver is the wood that is burnt by fire, but if it is burnt too much it becomes an untamable blaze capable of destroying everything both outside and within itself.

GALLBLADDER MERIDIAN

Twin meridian
Liver.

Season
Spring.

Element
Wood.

Solar time
11pm-1am.

Predominant emotion
Anger.

Feature
Twinned with the liver—a generator for the emotion of anger from the constructive point of view (fuel for doing) as well as the destructive one—the gallbladder deals with dosing this great power and is also the instrument through which the joyous element is emitted from the heart, the commissioner (client) of action.

Strengths
The balanced management of fear (possible through good functioning of the kidneys) is greatly beneficial to the gallbladder, which clearly shows an outstanding ability for decision-making as well as attention to detail. The gallbladder builds a person who is then able to elaborate the subsequent steps, one by one, necessary to overcome the dysfunction.

Weaknesses
With fear of action, the gallbladder becomes caught in a state of brooding. This leads to difficulty in digestion. The opposite of fear is love which, in Chinese culture, indicates joy for the wonderful things we are able to do. Looking at all of the body's meridians, it is easy to note how it is the meridian of the gallbladder which has the most points on the head, proving its huge influence on mental processes that tend to create a rather irrational and excessively meticulous mind, with a consequent hypo-functioning of one or more points of the meridian itself.

HEART MERIDIAN

Twin meridian
Small intestine.

Season
Summer.

Element
Fire.

Solar time
11am-1pm

Predominant emotion
Joy.

Feature
Traditional Chinese medicine sustains that the place inhabited by the spirit (*shen*, the divine spark) is found in the heart. And it is the heart itself that directs life at every level of existence, pushing people to evolve.

Strengths
Liveliness. Our life mission is understood in full as it is circulated by the heart meridian—the bridge between human and divine. The information produced by the heart is circulated throughout the entire body thanks to this meridian. The joy that is generated induces the individual to create through the liver-gallbladder meridian. A balanced heart is the perfect equilibrium between mind and emotion.

Weaknesses
Burning joy allows us to see the world through the eyes of love but, when the passion is exaggerated, reality is distorted.
If the heart meridian is out of balance, life is fast, but not lived to the full. Everything burns, but little remains. Another interesting nuance is the inability to accept others in unconditional love, thus giving rise to exploitation or sometimes psychological and physical abuse. Excessive joy is so excessive that it can hide a very deep sadness.

SMALL INTESTINE MERIDIAN

Twin meridian
Heart.

Season
Summer.

Element
Fire.

Solar time
1pm–3pm

Predominant emotion
Joy.

Feature
Working with its twin meridian, an interesting action occurs, similar to pumping, in which the heart pumps the blood and the small intestine —through peristalsis—elaborates the nutrients. In parallel, the intestine processes and absorbs transformed emotions and the heart sends them circulating in the body at a deep, cellular level. It's important to note how similar the brain and intestine are, both involved in managing emotions.

Strengths
Processing of emotions. This process is possible through the fire that the small intestine meridian unleashes releases both in a subtle and physical way in order to warm up the body and transform ingested foods and, therefore, in parallel, the emotions.

Weaknesses
What would happen if we didn't process our emotions? We wouldn't learn the lessons that they bring us, we would forever be at the mercy of events, without the ability to control them. The heart would be in perpetual turmoil, continually targeted by un-processed emotions, constantly subjected to electric shocks with arrhythmias and panic attacks. Over time, the heart would start to weaken due to exhaustion and subsequently lead the energic system into a powerful and inexorable crash, with inevitably extreme effects on health.

SPLEEN – PANCREAS MERIDIAN

Twin meridian
Stomach.

Season
End of the season.

Element
Earth.

Solar time
9-11am.

Predominant emotion
Worry.

Feature
The spleen-pancreas meridian together with the stomach deals in the transformation of energy.

Strengths
The ability to transform the densest energies in new, ready-to-use energy, makes the spleen a large container managing white globules, which could be described as the body's lines of defense where we learn to recognize the enemy, transforming it and making it flow into ready-for-use life energy.

Weaknesses
Malfunction in the spleen-pancreas meridian leads to the constant attempt to transform negative thoughts—a little like a very heavy meal waiting to be worked off. The continual attempt for conversion leads the cerebral cortex —connected to the meridian in question—to obsessive thoughts. Consequently, the emotional processing is blocked, always returning to the same starting point with a frustrating cyclical movement. The pancreas—which deals with the processing of sugar and therefore feelings, the sweetness of life—thus enters a mechanism of hyperfunctioning, going into overdrive. It is therefore normal in these conditions to ask for affection, or rather search for the sugary component, which will be used to placate said frustration. The higher the sugar level, the more the pancreas has to work, generating over time an even higher imbalance in the common meridian.

STOMACH MERIDIAN

Twin meridian
Spleen-pancreas.

Season
End of the season.

Element
Earth.

Solar time
7-9am.

Predominant emotion
Worry.

Feature
Together with the spleen and pancreas, the stomach has to do with the material, i.e., with real, tangible things; it therefore tells us of the possession and consequent management of the material world.

Strengths
The ability to be in a balanced relationship with the cycles of nature (and therefore of the Earth) both outside and within ourselves, contributing to a good functioning of the spleen-pancreas stomach meridian. The stomach is linked to the nervous system, therefore to our stress, which is maintained to an acceptable level when the stomach meridian is in equilibrium. It deals with nourishment, but also with the quality and ability to bring information and experiences from the outside, making life a place of fulfillment and personal growth.

Weaknesses
When events take over the emotions within ourselves without a clear logical answer. When we cannot understand the reason, the stomach enters a state of concern that it is unable to manage terrestrial events. The situation becomes indigestible as there is no rational logical response and therefore is no longer under our control or that of the people around us. One characteristic of the stomach meridian is that of sacrifice for others. An energy imbalance will tend to excessive sacrifice, for example forgetting about ourselves and putting ourselves second to the needs of others, inevitably generating a feeling of frustration and discomfort.

LUNG MERIDIAN

Twin meridian
Large intestine (colon).

Season
Fall.

Element
Metal.

Solar time
3-5am.

Predominant emotion
Sadness.

Feature
Organ that allows the direct exchange from inside to outside of the body and which deals with uniting the strength of energy from food with that of the *ki*, thereby favoring a balanced functioning of the body.

Strengths
The lungs bring us into contact with the outside world and help us exchange energies with others, to hold on or let go—just like the air we breathe—in any case in common with the other person. This meridian does not only deal with contact with the outside world, but also with bringing energies to every inch of the body and to keep the liquids circulating, like the lymphatic system which, among other things, expels metabolic waste from the body, leading them downwards in a balanced way from the top to the bottom of the body.

Weaknesses
An imbalance in the Lung Meridian is linked to our difficulty in holding on and/or letting go. It holds water, which is the symbol of the emotions we feel and which we are in contact with: any stagnation caused by physical and emotional retention, unregulated perspiration which is how we are supposed to release excess moisture and waste substances. An imbalance in the lungs is also responsible for constipation. The diaphragm tends to move less or block completely, reducing the opening of the lungs, which in turn take in little air and consequently little oxygen and *ki* so the body will nourish itself in an incorrect way. Too little energy means too little fuel and an imbalance in the physical and energic functioning.

LARGE INTESTINE (COLON) MERIDIAN

Twin meridian
Lung.

Season
Fall.

Element
Metal.

Solar time
5-7am.

Predominant emotion
Sadness.

Feature
Recognition and rejection of what is good and what is bad. To accept or to refuse?

Strengths
After the small intestine that deals with digestion and the acquisition of *ki* for the body comes the colon which has the important job of retaining and assimilating the liquid part of ingested food (which corresponds to the emotions). From here, the ability to accept or reject what is good or bad for ourselves, recognizing and not accepting what will be discarded as it carries waste. Just like with the lung that expands acquiring oxygen and *ki*, the large intestine is also an organ in movement, thanks to peristalsis which moves the nutrients down to the anus.

Weaknesses
What can be said about someone who seems nice, and clean on the outside, but who doesn't care about their inner being? Acne is often a symbol of an imbalanced intestine which, unable to purge itself of physical waste through correct fecal evacuation, activates a purification process through the skin. People with an extremely strong, rigid, and sometimes exaggerated attachment to ideals often hide problems at the colon meridian, which doesn't allow them to let go of their old beliefs in order to reconnect with new ones. Problems with this meridian have to do with excessive dry heat in various areas of the body.

MASTER OF THE HEART OR PERICARDIUM (HEART SUPPLEMENTARY) MERIDIAN

Twin meridian
Triple burner.

Season
Summer.

Element
Fire.

Solar time
7-9pm.

Predominant emotion
Emotional management.

Feature
The additional couple of the heart is dedicated to the management of fire, a place where feelings and emotions are separated and then sent to all the systems of the physical and subtle body.

Strengths
It is the deepest strength we have. The characteristic of this meridian is to ensure that the heart's functions are transmitted throughout the body, be they physical (like blood circulation) or psychological and subtle, such as fluid reasoning skills or the faculty of reconsidering our ideas, transforming, and adapting them. Irrigating the body in a capillary manner, we can be sure that our bodies are touched by pranic energy, the fuel of the chakras.

Weaknesses
When thought and action are less lucid, it means we are less able to find the most suitable solution. This meridian deals with sexuality linked to the concept of cosmic love and not the basest of impulses, but we can also find problems related to erections. Problems in blood circulation in one or several parts of the body alert us to difficulties in favoring the transformation of our animal side towards the more evolutionary celestial one.

TRIPLE BURNER (HEART SUPPLEMENTARY) MERIDIAN

Twin meridian
Master of the heart.

Season
Summer.

Element
Fire.

Solar time
9-11pm.

Predominant emotion
Emotional warmth.

Feature
Righteousness and wholeness as the equilibrium of our physical, emotional, psychological, and spiritual side.

Strengths
The supplementary heart meridian manages what comes from the outside—emotions, events—internalizing the sense and making it usable. It is defined "triple" because it deals with the three driving energies of being: our origins, which are deeply engrained into ourselves; our relationship with the Earth and matter; and finally, the way of the spirit, of our aptitude for the spiritualization (evolutionary transformation) of the reality around us. The equilibrium of these three energies equates to a life of full harmony and longevity. It also deals with the diffusion of heat throughout the body and emotions, therefore emotional temperament.

Weaknesses
From problems regarding nutrition in both the spiritual and physical sense, with the possibility of anorexia or bulimia, to the inability to listen to ourselves and our environments, which can lead to hearing issues. There are also problems regarding to phenomena of absence, when someone is often caught with their head in the clouds, preferring—more or less consciously—a place that is emotionally different than their present state, traveling elsewhere with their imagination.

the AURA

Y ou should start to understand now why it is so important to know about subtle physiology and how energy—our base fuel—flows through the etheric chakras, which channel it into the physical chakras, which then drive it to a cellular level via the systems of the dense body. None of this would be possible if the place where the etheric chakras are positioned—the auric body—did not exist.

The aura is the collection of a series of electromagnetic layers that surrounds the body of all beings of animate nature—human and animal—and of beings considered inanimate by science: plants and minerals. This scientific differentiation then tends to deteriorate in the eyes of the subtle observer, who sees life and movement in every being on Earth that has a more or less developed and extended aura and which vibrates, producing an atomic frequency or motion. In popular culture, the word "aura" is often used to describe a person with a more or less radiant temperament, whose aura is described as luminous; on the other hand, an aura can be said to be gray if the person in question is going through an emotionally difficult moment.

The four layers that are about to be illustrated link the living being to its original matrix of belonging, which we will find in the pages of this book under the name of cosmos.

The subtle and energic functioning that animates the physical body happens through the auric bodies: from basic energy to more subtle and sophisticated ones, to the emotions that only affect the physical body following the impressions generated by the mental body (which is not actually found in the brain, as we are led to believe), and before even then by the impulse of the causal body, which pushes the living being to have fulfilling experiences.

Thanks to the still-dormant potential that we have, humans could be the most naturally advanced being that planet Earth has ever seen!

Etheric Layer and Double Layer

Protection and boundaries are the central themes in a person's life, but just as important are the themes of contact and exchange, and both functions occur through the skin. Physical senses make us perceive the organ of the skin not only as a sensitive barrier against the environment around us, but also as an invisible border, indeed as a double protection, which will help us understand much about the role of the physical and subtle body, of the irrevocably essential bond between spirit and matter.

What are they?

They are two thin covering layers found near to the physical body.

Where are they?

The double is placed close to the physical body, covering it with a mantle about 0.4 inch thick. The etheric body encompasses the double body and the physical body; it is located at a distance of about 6 inches from the human body.

How do they work?

The two bodies are positioned in the same way as a protective screen since, like all subtle bodies, they are composed of a beam of electrons produced by human magnetism.

The double is the exact duplicate of the physical body, enveloping every single atom.

For the etheric body, on the other hand, we can imagine the environment in which we live as if it were permeated by many types of energy: those that are more material, and therefore also more visible, such as smog, pollution from factories, or soot let into the air by the flames of a burning fire, to then move on to those that humans cannot see: harmful fields such as, for example, the electromagnetic fields of radio and TV antennas, amplifiers, cell phones, and so on.

All these are forms of pollution that, as a result of prolonged exposure, can damage the functioning of subtle bodies and, therefore, consequently the physical one, creating disorders and pathologies that can influence the balanced conduct of daily life.

What would happen if you were directly exposed to all these agents?

What would happen to your health if you had no skin? If we had no double or etheric body, numerous problems would occur, problems making it impossible to live in this environment. This means that the functioning of the etheric body becomes indispensable for several reasons, the most obvious being that of protection and filtering of the dense and subtle energies of the outside world.

What are they for?

The etheric double performs innumerable activities so that the physical body and therefore the whole energy system can function in a balanced and interconnected way.

It absorbs pranic energy from the environment and then distributes it, through the chakras, in an extensive and balanced way throughout the body.

It has the important function of acting as a link, a bridge, between the physical body and the body after the etheric: i.e., the astral body.

We come into contact with the outside world through the dense body and through our senses we draw different impressions and reactions, which are then transmitted from the double to the astral body, which then, in a fast, perfectly synchronized manner, creates the relative emotional reactions. Inevitably, the double transmits to the astral body the consciousness of what is perceived from the outside world.

The etheric body is home to approximately 44,000 chakras which, for their subtle nature, could not survive immersed in a matrix of dense energies like the physical body does.

It supplies the physical body with energy during sleep and protects it from daily external energies: from the disturbing forces of parasitic entities

to natural and artificial electromagnetic ones. Contrary to what we may believe, the etheric body also defends against those excessively high energies which could in any case damage the nervous system. In Ancient Egypt, for example, during the rites that took place in the pyramids, initiates would perish from the energies of very high frequencies that the nervous system—although previously well prepared—was unable to absorb and transform for the use of the body.

This confirms how an excessive load of energy can be just as harmful as a deficiency.

Problems

Some issues related to an imbalance in the double or the etheric are very clear.

Stress, for example, is a category that encompasses several causes. Natural emotional events, tiredness, electromagnetism, a healthful diet but with low nutritional intake, a detachment from our spiritual side in favor of the psychological are the main reasons to look for in a malfunctioning of the double and the etheric, which can then affect all the subtle bodies above as well as the physical body below, altering their function.

Chronic fatigue is the first symptom to look into if the double is doing a poor job; it should in fact irrigate the body with new energy in a balanced way, allowing us to have a good night's sleep. There are many possible causes: just think how a bad diet can produce a level of energy that is inconsistent with the requirements of the energy system, which drives this energy to the storage centers that are not suitable for this type of energy, and which will then only use a part of it.

If you go to bed after midnight, your liver is unable to correctly exchange information with the cosmic matrix, which will send back unsuitable information to the subtle bodies, including data for the reconstruction or degeneration of the physical and subtle body.

Having insufficient energies, the double and the etheric will begin to lose thickness.

This thinning will cause a drop in the body's protection from external energies, meaning they will be able to take root in the physical body, leading to problems such as laceration in the layers; constant loss of energy, with a sensation of never-ending tiredness; and the entrance of low frequency energies which, inserting themselves inside the bodies, will begin to create profound disturbances, as they are not tolerated by the etheric body.

Cleansing and Harmonization

The double and the etheric body become dirty more frequently, since they are also responsible for protecting the dense body.

Environmental factors such as smog and dust agents can weigh them down, just as energy shortages or violent verbal assaults can often be the cause of injury, opening wounds and allowing energy parasites to take root.

Fumigation

The natural resin of the *Boswellia neglecta* plant can be used for cleaning both bodies. Place a few grains of resin on a pod of pressed charcoal (previously activated: i.e., set alight with a lighter or a match and placed in a special burner), and leave them to burn.

The smoke caused by the combustion must come into contact with the physical body (and consequently with the other bodies), which will whisper its request to cleanse and purify its auric bodies. This process is called fumigation.

You can then extinguish the charcoal in water, being careful not to throw it out while it is still active, or seemingly turned off.

Cleansing and suturing of the etheric body

To suture the etheric body, first you must always find the cause of the tear, in order to solve the problem at the root. Then proceed with your cleansing-and-suturing technique through a hyaline quartz, the tip of which must be used like you would use a scalpel.

Harmonization

Only then will the etheric body be treated with a manipulative technique in order to expand it and give it new breadth and energy capacity.

It is best to turn to an expert in the field for this procedure without improvising or guessing, which could—on the contrary—generate further damage or gravely worsen the symptoms, causing even more issues.

Astral or Emotional Layer

Emotions are the element that allows human beings to experiment with themselves in the world around them, evolving through the experiences lived.

Every emotion that manifests itself on the physical body is connected to one or more colors, which are the litmus paper testing the actual emotions felt by someone. The sudden variation of color based on the emotion felt is enough to amaze the observer.

What is it?

The emotional layer is also called the astral body and is the second layer of the auric system after that of the etheric double and the etheric body, which together make up a single body.

Where is it?

The emotional body is located between 10 and 20 inches away from the physical body, incorporating it together with the etheric double and the etheric body.

How does it work?

In any situation that human beings go through in life, they experience different kinds of emotions and impressions, from the slightest feelings that we perhaps do not even notice—for example, the stress caused by living in a big city with loud noises—to the most powerful that touch us in a more visible way. Most people are now used to putting up with this type of emotion, as we are not as inclined to listen to ourselves; but emotions affect first the psyche and then the body, generating problems in both the medium and long term.

Emotions that the physical body endures due to symptoms silenced by the intake of chemical drugs will subsequently transform into different types and entities of pathology. We must now understand how this reaction takes place and where it comes from.

Commonly, the primary emotions are considered innate and universal. From research carried out over the last two decades, it has been ascertained that emotional creation takes place primarily in the homonymous layer, which changes color based on the emotion experienced, to then be transformed into a physical emotion through the brain as it receives the decryption command.

We understand, therefore, how important this layer is for our psychophysical and relational well-being.

Learning to see and hear auras can also be of use in preventing symptoms and illnesses that pass through the etheric body before they manifest in the physical one.

They are therefore subtle pieces of data that remain in the emotional body for a certain period.

What is it for?

The astral or emotional body is the connecting bridge between the physical brain and the mind. It is found in one of the subtle bodies: the psychological layer. This means that the brain is simply an executor of commands received from the mind.

Thanks to the astral body, it is possible to experience the full range of emotions that allow human beings to evolve, turning them into life experience.

The astral body elaborates denser, baser—you could even say primitive—emotions, or more refined and therefore more evolved ones, depending on the level of evolution.

Depending on the type of personal evolution, the astral body allows us to experience emotions of a different nature, which can only be understood based on their stage of development. It is therefore impossible to make someone understand a particularly high emotion if they are not evolved enough.

It then becomes apparent that the physical body cannot perceive sensations, the beauty of life, a moving and exciting event, without the astral body: without an astral body, human beings would basically be automatons.

The peculiar feature of the astral body is how colors suddenly change, depending on the emotions that are projected onto the physical body through the mind and then the brain.

The emotional body tells the truth, whereas the human character may try to lie or change deeply ingrained traits to appear different, better, or more acceptable in the eyes of others, enacting a behavior that is different from the reality.

The astral body instead speaks of what we are, deep down. If everyone were gifted to see others' astral bodies, what kind of society would we be living in?

Problems

When we are asleep, the dense body rests so that it can regenerate its own vital energies, while the subtle bodies are in full activity.

Through the astral body, journeys are embarked on in which the conscience is able to travel enormous distances in minimal periods of time, bringing significant advantages for evolutionary purposes.

When the astral layer separates, its space is occupied by astral energy from the environment outside, allowing the energy system to function normally.

However, the energy that has taken over is often heavy or not very clean, frequently because of where the person chooses to sleep, which could be inhabited by energies polluted by those who were there before them, or from memories left there—or even from unhealthy electromagnetic currents.

At this point, a problematic energy is established, within the auric bodies, which overloads the energy system, sometimes bringing parasites that feed on the astral energy rather than letting it reach the system itself.

This then causes a problem in returning from the astral journey, as the original astral substance finds an environment that is polluted and dirty. It will therefore have difficulty in realigning itself with other bodies and, upon awakening, we will find it complicated, and at first scary, to move our physical body.

All symptoms fade in time; the regenerated astral energies allow us to slowly take possession of our bodies, and therefore return to ordinary life.

Hence the need to live in an environment that is physically and energetically clean, where all of our activities, both awake and asleep, can become a highly restorative and evolutionary experience.

Cleansing and Harmonization

The astral body can run into several problems. One regards auric lacerations, which can occur on the double and etheric body—due, for example, to an unhealthy lifestyle—which can be resolved by changing lifestyle through fumigation or ether-suturing.

The most suitable resin for this astral layer is *Boswellia sacra,* which is fumigated close to the astral body with the deep request of purging it from any parasites that have taken root.

Other problems can arise during astral travel in people who, not rooted enough to the Earth, or without an emotional center, tend to flee from their emotions. These individuals are like a tree with short roots, one that risks being felled at the merest hint of a strong wind (or emotion). To avoid the powerful, yet evolutionary, world of emotions, some people choose to take refuge in their mind—an idealized and often imagined place—thus excluding everything practical and everyday that may put them to the test and make them evolve in the world.

Upon returning from astral travel, someone with this trait risks running into problems of reentry into the physical body, because, as mentioned already, emotions flee to the thinnest planes most distant from the Earth, thereby developing the desire to stay sheltered, disconnected, to never return, hiding in the subtle world—which, however, is not suitable for a long stay. The human astral body is not built for letting the physical body go for prolonged periods: an overly long stay can lead to several problems—energic first, physical second.

It is therefore recommended we only approach the development of the astral body when we are harmoniously grounded in the Earth and have a balanced general management of our emotions.

Mental
Layer

Over the centuries, after experiments and research on the mind within the physical body, we have confirmed that there is no trace of it. The ancient Egyptians believed that the brain performed a servile function, which is why it was eliminated during mummification. By dissecting it, we have lost all certainty that the mind is located in the brain.

Nowadays, in fact, we are more convinced that the mind is actually to be found outside of the brain.

But where, exactly? In the thin layer dedicated to it—that is, the mental body.

What is it?

The mental body is the third layer of the auric body, starting from the physical one.

Where is it?

It is approximately two feet from the physical body. It is ovoid in shape but does not occupy the entire structure in a uniform manner.

How does it work?

It is the stratification that houses the higher ego in its part of concrete thought, the part of the energy system that requires the human being to evolve. The latter is found in the causal body; however, it cannot act from here on direct instructions of the physical body; rather it collaborates with it in reaching a type of functioning that is linked to abstract-theoretical thought.

Through the mental body the higher ego can instead put into action its strategies on the actions of the physical body, pushing it to live experiences to make the person evolve. Therefore, the mental body becomes the subtle body which acts as a bridge between the causal body and the astral one—meaning that consequently the etheric body will allow the abstract form to become concrete action.

Over the ages, human beings have developed an auric layer for each one.

The Atlantean civilization, for example, learned how to structure the astral body and, therefore, to manage the emotions, creating great opportunities for growth—but also immense disasters.

In the modern era, however, it was the mental body that was structured to learn the lesson of love and aid toward others, rather than destruction and oppression. Today the mental body has developed early in one part of its functions: we just need to think about our struggles for equality and inclusion—which, however, in my opinion are sometimes exploited and aimed at causing more confusion, while others are typical of the evolution that the mental body must go through: i.e., unconditional love.

What is it for?

Its name gives us a clue to its role: it regards concrete thought, the reasoning behind the actions of the physical body. The mental body merges a person's data with those arriving from the outside, thus creating impressions which, intertwined, allow reasoning and critical thinking.

Not all areas of this body, however, are active, and therefore some need to be developed, such as, for example, a propensity for the arts. The mental body, in fact, deals with imagination, memory, and all qualities associated with them. Imaginative capacity allows us to realize our thoughts and projects more quickly.

The mental body also has the important function of drawing information from the experiences of the physical body, which are integrated with those related to personal evolution, which are kept in the causal body.

During its various incarnations, moreover, it gifts a very precise conscience which imposes an averagely evolved human being to carry out certain decisions and avoid others. This body type also creates the synthesis thought-forms of ways of thinking that affect our personal life:

those of a positive nature—love, hope, faith—attract benevolent aspects, which in the current language are defined as functional; on the other hand, when we experience thoughts of fear, hatred, or vengeance, they reverberate on other beings—just as positive thoughts do—attracting the corresponding dysfunctional result.

Finally, it is important to understand how the mental body also works through a marked scientific intelligence—which, in order to properly and fully evolve, has to learn to integrate empathy and love, emotions that often fall short.

Problems

A human being with a developed mental body is capable of realizing what are called "wonders" by those still in the awakening phase.

The mental body deals with thought, radiating it everywhere and affecting living beings. The problem lies in the way of thinking: humans, in fact, are a powerful transmitter and receiver of thought. Just think, for example, of how joy can be contagious when a large group of people gathers together to achieve a common goal.

Unfortunately, it is also possible that positive thoughts alternate with negative ones—first of all, fear: for example, the wave of general dismay that arises when people receive harmful news constantly and daily, pushed toward taking action that, before that certain event, they considered unthinkable.

Fear and other similar feelings act in the same way as a wave of joy: the mental body produces the thought-forms or egregores. These make up the ability to think in a certain way for long periods of time, a method that produces a change in the quality of human life as we start to attract events of the same quality of thought, nourishing the egregore itself. Therefore, we witness the events of people who live in fear and live a life marked and terrified by perennial suffering.

Individual thought-forms exist, but when multiple people express them at the same time we are witnessing a collective egregore that can cover neighborhoods, cities, countries, and even the entire world, bending people who don't listen to themselves to the request contained in the thought-form.

Thought-forms, however, can also develop positively, if based on the most powerful feeling in the world: love.

Cleansing and Harmonization

It is possible to harmonize the mental body by evolving one's modality of thought. In the current period of incarnations, human beings are being called on to do just that.

Self-knowledge starts from a sufficient self-perception as to be able to understand our own mode of self-sabotage.

Inner saboteurs are those who prefer to avoid the best for themselves, heading, through inner obstacles, toward other situations. The lower ego—that part of the personality that lives unbalanced, in power or in ambition, and that does not wish to change—believes that these are more productive, habitual, or, at some level, salvific compared to the area of comfort that the person will have to go beyond to effect a change.

Recognizing the path we are on when we sabotage ourselves is the first step on the road to change.

It is the same with thought-forms of a heavy nature. It is therefore necessary to become as aware as possible of who we are and how we function in order to be able to act. When we start to understand that living in fear leads to nothing, but it actually leads to a greater and faster decay—for example, when we understand that watching a horror movie or gorging on junk TV is harmful and we begin to prefer the idea of a healthier lifestyle immersed in nature, choosing what to nourish ourselves with in every sense—that is the first step. Disassembling an egregore, turning it positive, is only possible when all negative thoughts are transformed, visualizing the heavy ones as burned and replacing them with those of a benevolent nature.

You just need to look for information to make this possible: there is a lot of very inspirational material out there.

Causal
Layer

Accessing the causal body allows us to confront the most striking and charming of the four subtle bodies. Its functions place the human being in a continuous, constant line among past, present, and future.

This reference system, however, is merely a human convention, a stratification that allows us to understand how people are overall small, complex—but with an almost infinite potential—bearers of the divine flame.

What is it?

The causal body is the layer farthest from the physical body. It is a container that generates events within people, allowing the deep self (the superior ego) to evolve through experiences lived and subsequently consolidated.

Where is it?

It is placed about 60 inches from the physical body and incorporates the previous three bodies: double and etheric, astral, and psychological. This layer is connected to all other bodies, and generates the causes of those events that occur in and around the person: for example, pathologies (which always occur for the purpose of an evolutionary message) or external events in general.

How does it work?

This is where the subject, the proponent, takes full responsibility for those events that occur. The context or external subjects do not have direct responsibilities, contrary to what we are sometimes inclined to think. Our causal body therefore asks for experience, resolution, and evolution.

Of all the subtle bodies allocated to people who incarnate, the causal one is the only one that remains the same in all incarnations, while the previous bodies tend to break up during the physical departure. People therefore are given a new double and etheric, astral, and mental body with each incarnation.

The causal body contains the memory of all previous incarnations, of each experience that the person has lived; it forms the inclinations of the personality that each individual maintains throughout their life and which they will develop based on past experiences.

This body contains all the future qualities that a person must develop in the present and subsequent incarnations.

What is it for?

In the beginning, primitive, unevolved people, with basic, prehistoric behaviors and emotions, had dormant causal bodies, as no experiences had been lived to allow for progress. Moving on, according to the theory of seeds that must sprout in the present incarnation, the causal body generates the events and experiences that will nourish it, allowing a gradual awakening. The more the causal body is nourished and therefore awakened, the more the individual will be evolved and aimed toward the good, as if they were full of light to spread in a benevolent way around themselves.

The awakening of the causal body begins when someone undertakes a path of discovery of the profound truth and, generally, can last for many incarnations to come.

The primary qualities of happenings that are able to awaken this body are thoughts and actions undertaken for others: in this way, we leave our own individual ego to discover a mechanism of altruistic behavior.

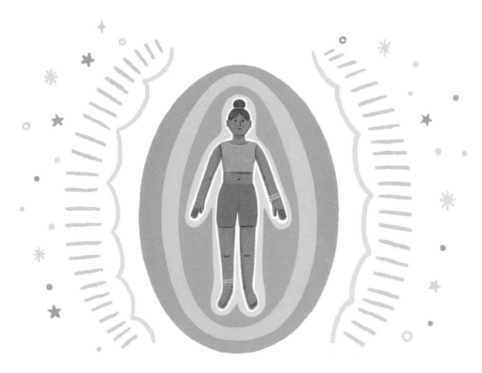

The causal body coordinates all other bodies, separating and storing the most useful information through the physical body which acts, the astral one that deals with emotions, and the psychological one that deals with the thought behind what actually happens.

But not all emotions end up stored in the causal body: for example, base sexuality, fury, and pride are purged, as the causal body can only take on the brightest, most positive part of those experiences that people go through and undertake over the course of their incarnations.

From this layer comes the power of deep meditation with its benefits.

Magic, interpreted by the outside world as an inexplicable event, is generated by the awakened causal body through a wise use of the same.

Problems

A human being in its first incarnations is characterized by a causal body that is without color and almost inactive.

The causal layer itself is only capable of storing the events and positive impressions perceived during a lifetime, and not the bad deeds that reside in the memory.

Nonetheless, issues can arise within a wicked person—for example, those who over numerous years of study are initiated into the theoretical and practical knowledge of subtle mechanisms and use them to hinder the seed of absolute good that is theirs at birth.

During childhood, and especially up to fourteen years of age, it is important that children be taught by their parents' example about altruism and goodness in general. If not, that seed of goodness is likely—especially in cases of major family trauma and negative experiences—to bow to evil.

Activated after years of research and study, it is as if the causal body were the prey of the egoic personality of the individual to subjugate others, using two great powers: sex and money.

This is how dark witches and wizards are born, those who use their causal body for so-called black magic.

Although it would be logical to think that such people are insensitive to the pain that they cause, the truth is that they are fully aware of it, indoctrinated and initiated into the laws of the occultism they use for reasons that often have to do with their own past marked by darkness and fear.

It is important therefore that parents educate their children, not only for social reasons, but also to develop people who in the future will have been brought up in love, goodness, and light.

Cleansing and Harmonization

In my opinion, it is pointless to speak of cleansing the causal body, as the causal body is not inclined to get dirty in any way. Information on the surrounding environment provided by the senses is purified in advance by the previous subtle bodies.

It is more appropriate to look into the development of the causal body, which can be done over time through study and self-knowledge.

Choosing a very deep path implies the study of techniques related to the knowledge of subtle bodies: for example, theosophy, which boasts Helena Blavatsky, founder of the theosophical society, Rudolf Steiners, and Arthur Edward Powell. This doctrine deals with the understanding of the subtle world, helping people awaken their own consciousness and develop their evolutionary seed—the higher ego—by studying the laws of cosmic

nature, which regulate and permeate both the external and internal environment, as we can learn through the study of subtle bodies, the functioning of subtle anatomy, and the physiology of the human being: a journey that is very simply introduced in the pages of this book.

As well as study, we can also embark on self-discovery and -growth through a series of initiations toward knowledge, allowing us to consciously develop and activate our subtle bodies to the maximum, all the way to the causal one.

This is a journey that naturally changes during the various incarnations and accelerates its evolution; it is important to find the right teachers to guide us, teachers who are capable and always working toward what is best for others, whether they are human or not.

Frequencies

I often hear frequencies being talked about in the most wide-ranging of fields, from music to physics. Within the energic system—and inevitably in the physical one—it is considerably important and useful for us to know them and understand their function, also based on the speed at which they propagate.

Depending on the function they have to perform, every system, organ, and, ultimately, cell vibrates at different speeds, which allows them to carry out their tasks, keeping the physical body alive.

Where are they, and how do they work?

The Treccani Italian dictionary defines *frequency* as "the number of times that a periodic phenomenon repeats in the unit of time."

Every living being is made up of electromagnetic fields, just as the Earth is.

Anyone with the gift can see the auric field, particularly the astral one, with its colors that quickly change depending on the emotions felt by the person. This range consists of atoms which, vibrating at certain speeds, and therefore frequencies, appear in different color tones. The slower the vibrations, the colors we see are predominantly red or orange; while, as the vibrations increase in speed, we see more colors like purple and white. These remind us, not surprisingly, of the colors of the physical chakras, and we can notice how the colors that vibrate more slowly deal with denser, more physical qualities, while the faster ones present more subtle and spiritual attitudes.

Low frequencies correspond to dense quality emotions such as fear, while the higher frequencies correspond to joy and the highest of all emotions: love.

Fear tends to block energy, stopping its flow, as anyone who has suffered a panic attack knows all too well; love, on the other hand, lets it flow and allows for energies of movement, of revolution: just think of how much energy you have when you are in love, all the things you are able to do! If, however, we find ourselves living in a constant state of fear, we are more prone to disease, due to the fact that our immune system vibrates more slowly when we are anxious, meaning we are unable to fight off simple viruses or bacteria. Is it really worth living in fear? What is the price to pay?

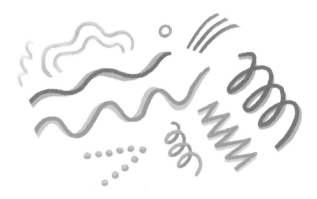

Colors and Vibrations:
Examples of Frequency

A very interesting example of colors in relation to vibratory frequencies is made up of the aura. Each auric layer tends to glow in one or more colors, according to the wearer.

The astral layer shines with vivid, bright colors when someone is experiencing the highest and subtlest emotions such as love, joy, or devotion; while the shades turn dark when experiencing low emotions such as anger or fear. They also change according to someone's evolutionary stage: in this case, the most primitive.

Through the interpretation of subtle bodies, if we look at a photograph taken with a special camera, or through the eyes of a careful observer, we can understand ourselves, our own emotions, or the nature of our own evolutionary situation.

In the astral body, colors refer to specific emotions, the most common of which are:

✦ cloudy black, corresponding to malice or hatred;

✦ dark red on a black base, evoking anger;

+ blood red, corresponding to sensuality;

+ very dark green, which refers to jealousy—green refers to a propensity to others, a brilliant tone to great vitality;

+ very thick mixed gray, expressing fear;

+ bright pink, expressing unconditional, free love;

+ red with blue (crimson) undertones, which refers to a selfish love;

+ orange, which speaks of pride and ambition;

+ yellow, which tells of intellectual inclinations;

+ blue, which highlights religious or spiritual inclination or devotion;

+ purple, which testifies to a devotion and affection for what one truly believes in.

Generally speaking, the brighter the colors, the higher and purer the inclinations: it is therefore impossible to hide from the true, deep photograph of our emotional selves.

Channels and Perceptual Tools

Human beings are made up of different types of frequencies, which generate electromagnetic fields between them that can be perceived in different ways.

The auric body is a vibrational field—visible to a trained eye—which can be felt and measured not only by our own hands, but also using the invaluable pendulum.

Palming

Hands have always been a very sensitive tool. Palming is the ability to use your hands to listen to the subtle energies of animate and inanimate beings.

When two people meet, they feel a series of impressions as they get closer to each other. These impressions make up the sensation known as "instinct."

As we have already determined, the skin is the first energic covering, the etheric double, which receives information on its way to the brain, decodifying them on the physical body.

When two individuals become intimate, their subtle bodies touch, exchanging information. This is what happens, for example, during "love at first sight," in which the auric layers identify that particular experience in the other person that, on the evolutionary level, they need and which they will be able to experience through that person.

You can try palming by bringing your hand to about 8 inches from your body, starting preferably from a dense area, such as the abdomen or chest. Then start making small movements back and forth; this will help you start to feel something, such as heat, or cold at a certain density, almost as if you were finding it difficult to continue: this sensation signals the start of your etheric body. If your etheric body is too close to the physical one, and if you can also feel a slight sensation of density with your hand, this is indicative of an overly subtle and unhealthy layer, under stress, with a physical body that is more prone to frequent illness.

A healthy etheric body should be about 6 inches away from the physical body.

You can then proceed in various areas of the body and on the different subtle bodies, starting from a distance slightly greater than those indicated in the chapter on auric layers.

The Pendulum

The pendulum is an investigative tool that can complement or replace palming, sometimes making it more detailed.

From the simplest kind, made with a thread and a button, to the more complicated in various materials, the pendulum oscillates over the body, connecting it with the causal body that holds the most interesting information, acquiring it through the cosmic vibrational field. This system is able to provide us with a variety of data, such as the state of the subtle bodies, any tears, parasites, and so on.

Before use, you need to first decide how to decode the direction of the motion: for example, clockwise to indicate yes and counterclockwise for no. You can permanently imprint a certain movement code through meditation and informing your superior ego, where the causal body is found, repeating your decision in depth. Then hold the pendulum, in a pinching grip between the fingers, keeping the wrist limp and asking it to move alone, indicating yes (clockwise) and no (counterclockwise).

It is always best to start with simple questions, without influencing them with your mind through any movement of the wrist: for example, asking if the glass in front of you is full and then asking the opposite, if the glass is empty. When the answer is correct, you can continue with other, more complicated exercises. After good training (there is no need to rush!), you can start with questions regarding the subtle bodies and their state of health. It's good practice to always ask the opposite question to check the answers, in order to keep your mind from influencing the pendulum's movement.

It requires time and practice to perfect this technique, without rushing as said above, and keeping under control any frustration that may arise.

PRACTICES AND REMEDIES TO HARMONIZE CHAKRAS AND THE AURA

The auric body and the chakras give rise to frequencies and, consequently, to energy. Several internal factors—above all, emotional ones—alter the frequencies of our bodies, causing varying kinds of disturbances: in the worst scenario, disease. There are, however, some active, effective precautions we can take, from prevention to stable re-equilibrium.

Seeing Them and Hearing Them

The cosmos is based and built on frequencies. Let's take colors as an example: while looking at a rainbow, we could wonder how it is possible to see so many different colors so close together.

From red to indigo, each color vibrates at different atomic speeds. So, while the atoms of the color red move at a certain speed, purple vibrates at a much higher rate.

One simple test involves taking a red pen and swinging it very fast, shaking your wrist. You will be able to observe how, the quicker it moves, the more the color tends to transform from red to another color; on the other hand, the slower the movement, the more the pen returns to its original color.

We can see both the auric body and the chakras in the same way. Humans are also made of frequencies: the quicker they vibrate, the more easily the eyes—with a little training—will be able to capture what they normally wouldn't see.

It is therefore possible to touch the subtle bodies by placing one hand toward one of them and listening to the sensations that arrive: in this way, we are able to perceive the density of an auric layer—the breadth, cleanliness, and any bumps, which are the indicators of a very precise energic system.

Similarly, it is possible to feel the activity of a chakra by placing one hand near it, without touching the physical body, and listening to what kind of sensations arrive: hot, cold, tingling, tremors, and, if we pay more attention, even the emotional part linked to the chakra such as joy, sadness, or anger, and so on.

The ability to see the chakras depends on the sensitivity of the observer themselves and which frequency vibrates the most when based on a healthy lifestyle, on study, and on the knowledge of the subtle world.

Exercises to Visualize the Subtle

There are several exercises to improve your vision and contact with the subtle world. However, we must be aware that not everyone has the same ability to see and hear, because of the structural diversity of human beings: we are all similar, but no two are the same.

The first point to take into consideration is lifestyle, in particular our nutrition—both in a physical and psychic sense.

The philosopher Ludwig Feuerbach (1804–1872) asserted, with very good reason, that "we are what we eat." Nothing is more true, considering how healthful eating produces energy with high vibrations. Likewise, it is also important to understand what we feed on emotionally through the lifestyle we choose. Regular use of video games or horror movies, an exclusive interest in what is faraway and outside of ourselves, excluding nature: these are all ways of keeping your frequencies down.

It is a good idea, therefore, to live as healthy a lifestyle as possible, through self-knowledge, observation of nature and its teachings, to the interior discovery, allowing you to discover your darker sides that you can then resolve and evolve. Meditation, for example, is a good path to self-knowledge. It's just as important to spend as much time surrounded by nature as possible, taking it slow, at least from time to time, as it is to purify the body, for example through fasting, but always under the guidance of an expert and for short periods of time.

A return to self helps us raise our frequencies and remains the only way to access the subtle worlds.

Zazen Meditation

This particularly effective and simple technique to rebalance the chakras and subtle bodies originates from Japan. For ease of use, here are some practical instructions for simplified application.

You will need

+ a meditation mat.

+ 1 white or blue candle.

+ lighter/matches.

+ music for meditation.

Time

+ 15 minutes.

+ every day, or whenever possible.

Instructions

+ Turn off your cell phone and make sure you are not disturbed.

+ Sit on the floor on a mat.

+ Turn on relaxing music.

+ Place a lighted candle in front of you, about 3 feet away.

+ Breathe in through your nose and out through your mouth for 3–4 minutes, relaxing the body. Starting from your feet to your head, try to eliminate all thoughts. When thoughts arise, ask them kindly to leave.

+ Look into the candle flame. Stare at it, trying to blink as little as possible. After a few minutes, you will probably feel like you are slowly entering the flame, becoming part of it.

+ Stay in this state for at least 10 minutes. You will notice that your thoughts will ease for a short time, leaving you in a state of emptiness. This is the core of meditation: creating a condition of vacuum.

What happens

Over time, this practice will allow the mind to be harmonized by giving you a sense of well-being that you will eventually find yourself searching for every day.

Meditation allows you to gradually detoxify the aura from stagnant energies, giving space to higher—and therefore healthier—frequencies.

By raising your frequencies, you allow the auric body to expand and consequently enhance its energy. In some cases, it even repairs cuts or tears in the aura. Thus you will reach a high level of self-awareness.

Breathing

Breathing is the very first action a human performs involuntarily. Without air, there is no life.

You can check the quality of your breathing through one very simple test. Stand up. Inhale deeply through the nose, taking in as much air as possible. If you feel the air flow, deeply inflating your chest and abdomen, then your diaphragm—the organ that makes sure oxygen reaches your lungs—is most probably working well enough. If, on the other hand, you can feel the air blocked after just a few seconds without fully inflating your lungs, then the diaphragm probably isn't working as well as it should.

What causes us to breathe little and badly?

We tend to hold our breath when we are scared. Living in a constant state of fear of illness, war, lack of money: all these things can emotionally influence the diaphragm. Looking more deeply, this means little air is allowed in to protect us from external—sometimes presumed—dangers, and from dangerous external dynamics: it can therefore reasonably be considered a protection measure.

Cardiac Coherence 365 breathing is a medically approved method which allows us to release stress and fear, thereby allowing the diaphragm muscle to soften. In this way, the chakras are able to pump energy in a more balanced way, permitting the auric bodies to remodel their functionality.

Instructions for cardiac coherence

position

+ Standing or sitting.

Time

+ 5 minutes, 2–3 times a day.

Instructions

+ Inhale through the nose for 5 seconds to fully inflate the abdomen.

+ Exhale through your mouth for 5 seconds to completely deflate the abdomen.

+ Continuing to inhale and exhale, count the 5 seconds (in your head or on your fingers) as if following the hands of a clock.

Visualization

Visualizing or imagining remains one of the best ways to see changes occurring around us in the world.

From meditation to more advanced balancing techniques, it is important that you visualize the change you want to see happen. There are, however, some very important rules you must follow if you want visualization or imagination to work.

You will need

+ Meditation chair or mat.

Time

+ Few minutes.

Instructions

+ First, what you want to achieve can arise from the mind, helping you to see it better (perfect function for the third eye).

+ Then it has to be carried forward, visualizing it through the heart and circulating it throughout the body at a deep and cellular level, with passion.

+ The last step is to feel the change in the solar plexus (a nervous and energic center found below the diaphragm), letting it go, visualizing it until it is absorbed by the space above your head—i.e., by the cosmos.

Test

+ Imagine that your chakras are all balanced.

+ Visualize your own auric field slowly reassembling, stitching itself back together and thickening; see yourself in full health and with lots of vitality; try to imagine as many details as possible.

+ Move this visualization or image to the heart chakra along with the deepest reason why you want it. Feel it strongly, in a powerful way.

+ Take this whole process to the solar plexus, which, just like a powerful catapult, entrusts the visualization to the cosmos.

Repeat the various steps several times during the day—but never only use the mind—completing the above steps in quick succession.

You can do visualization with your eyes open or closed, and in any situation or environment.

Suggestion

Finally, I would like to make a brief statement about our young children. Let them daydream: they are passing down one of the most important lessons we have to learn, one that belongs to them in an innate—and still rather intact—manner.

Stones

With the term "stones," I refer to crystals, and to fossil resins such as amber and ammonite, all of which are invaluable in helping to rebalance the chakras but also perfect for auric bodies.

You will need

+ Yellow-colored or dark amber-colored amber, and/or natural kyanite crystal.

Time

+ Based on your feelings.

Instructions

+ The stones can be passed over the etheric double or the etheric body of the areas to be treated, visualizing the heavy energies you want to remove as they pass. It's good to listen to yourself and maybe repeat the process all over again until you feel the treated area is once again balanced with the rest of the body.

+ It is vital to finish the treatment by visualizing throwing away the heavy energies collected by the stone into the fire at your feet, imagining that they are burned, and then shake the stone as if you were resetting an old thermometer.

It is also good to remember to clean the stones from any energies still attached, arranging them on an amethyst druse (set of purple crystals) for at least 72 consecutive hours away from direct sunlight. The amethyst will lighten all the energies carried by the stones. Cleansing stones is a complex task that changes from stone to stone. It is therefore good for beginners to avoid using water, salt, or anything else that could damage them, and to favor the amethyst as a universal method, which can also be used to cleanse unwanted energies from any substance or object as well as cleansing stones.

I recommend using amber as a gentle cleaner. If you notice that some areas are harder to clean, you can resort to kyanite.

Spray

Subtle bodies and chakras are very sensitive to external frequencies. One natural aid is an aqueous solution that can be used near the auric bodies.

The solution includes different elements, such as plant extracts, flowers, gems, and sometimes stones. Bach or Australian flowers can be added, as well as essential oils, and various other substances of vegetable origin. To be able to choose the correct elements, you will need to study—in depth—each one's properties and their combined reactions, connecting them to whatever goal you have set yourself.

Instructions

+ We need a spray that dissolves heavy energies on contact with the physical or subtle bodies or chakras. We then use the stones to remove these energies or let them release into the surrounding environment naturally. It is, therefore, better to perform the cleansing outside rather than indoors, to avoid having to perform a further cleansing.

✦ Spray the mixture approximately 16 inches around the physical body, asking the spray to cleanse it. If you are even slightly sensitive, you should be able to tell that it is working by feeling a fresh, light sensation—maybe even a shiver.

These preparations can even benefit the environments in which we live. I personally produce this solution for subtle bodies, the preparation of which requires a very long list of ingredients.

Suggestion

There are a number of products available on the market. I would like to especially recommend Serapis Bey by Aura-Soma and Ambiente Purity by Australian Bush Flowers Essence. These sprays are suitable for the environments in which we live and work, which are often full of unwanted energies brought from outside and/or mostly generated by fear, stress, and anxiety.

Nature

Nature plays a central role in people's well-being. Living in urban centers has made us forget the countless benefits that a healthful environment can bring.

Time

+ The duration of this exercise depends solely on your own sensitivity.

Instructions

+ To help you on your first endeavor in Forest Therapy, one of the first exercises is to choose a tree that you find particularly appealing.

+ Moving slowly, and if possible barefoot, place your hands on the trunk, visualizing roots coming out of your feet and sinking about five feet into the earth and expanding farther and farther outward.

+ Start to breathe, inhaling through the nose and exhaling through the mouth. On each exhale, let all your unwanted heavy energies seep out through your mouth and feet. On every inhale, visualize pure white transparent light energy pouring in through the top of your head to gradually replace the heavy energies as they leave.

+ During this process, ask the tree for assistance in the transformation. The tree has a circuit, similar to the human lymphatic system, which absorbs part of the heavy energies, discharging them into the ground, where they will become nourishment for the forest.

+ Finally, embrace the tree, placing your chest and genitals fully in contact with the trunk, resting your cheek, and breathing in the beneficial substances it produces. You will hear more peace within you, and you will find a sensation of calm and lightness.

+ As it is a living being and an invaluable helper, we should always remember to thank the tree for its work.

For this kind of exercise, it is ideal to find somewhere far away from sources of pollution: smog, electromagnetism, noise, etc. Alternatively, even a tree in a city park will do just fine. We have to make do with what we have!

Illness: Chakras and Subtle Bodies

T he message of disease arrives through an imbalance in energy, mainly created by incorrect behavioral patterns and malnutrition.

Causes are often sequential, as we are what we eat and how we live. Assisting the causal body that generates illness with the aim of looking for an evolutionary solution for the person involved is one of the greatest gestures of love that the cosmos can enact. All so human beings can evolve.

Why do we get sick

The word *pathology* comes from the Greek *pàthos*, which refers to both disease—or suffering—and deep feeling, emotions, and contact with the self.

What does such a frightening element as illness have to do with deep feeling? It is correct to assert that pathologies arise from listening incorrectly, that they alert us to one or more situations of daily life in which we are undertaking a dysfunctional behavior pattern that is lacking in love.

Illness originates from a series of mechanisms put in place by the causal body in order to bring attention to whichever is the imbalanced pattern that needs to be corrected.

It is, therefore, important to stop considering illness merely as an event of pain and death, and rather to perceive it as a message to be taken seriously and understood.

This kind of message can be listened to and acted upon through my *Riconoscere, Risolvere, Praticare* (*Recognize, Resolve, Practice*, or RRP) methods that I teach during my training courses:

+ the first R, *Recognize*, corresponds to the phase in which we become aware that a message exists and start to recognize it, relating it to the moments it is put into practice every day. Should we be unable to interpret the message, a course of soul psychosomatics is recommended, as is a consultation with a specialist;

+ the second R, *Resolve*, sees the dysfunctional pattern undergo a deep transformation following a change in attitude in our behavior;

+ finally, the P for *Practice* introduces a new behavioral pattern, overwriting the old one and therefore becoming the new everyday normal.

With this in mind, it would perhaps be more appropriate to replace the terrible word "illness" with one that is undoubtedly more joyful and loving: *wellness*.

The Mechanisms that Generate Disease

When we continue to live even just some aspects of our life in a way that is not in harmony with the cosmic laws, the mechanism of wellness comes into being.

The mental body begins to produce thoughts to make us reflect on our behavioral dynamics.

Theoretically, at this stage we should be able—within reason—to change those dynamics and thereby subconsciously avoid illness arising.

However, sometimes, due to incapacity or a lack of will, we ignore the message, which then is passed to the underlying subtle body, the astral or emotional body. In this phase, the causal body induces impulses which start affecting us on an emotional level, initially through "random" messages—for example, in books or films—to then move on

to manifestations of disharmony through more important events, such as disputes, arguments, and so on.

If we continue to ignore these signals, they move on to the next body, the etheric one, where these events become more explicit and powerful, often erroneously convincing us that it is merely to do with bad luck.

When mild symptoms occur, if the message continues to be ignored, there is nothing left but the physical wellness solution, which will connect with the organ of reference and cause the illness relating to the issue to be solved.

We are then left with two choices: first, to fight the symptoms and/or illness itself, silencing the message, with a consequent, even more urgent, effect on other organs; or, second, to identify the signal, make the right change—something that can be done at almost every stage of the illness, even following surgical intervention—to avoid the issue recurring.

Understanding the Messages of Illness

Wellness only requires us to solve its own dysfunctional part, and the RRP system is one effective way of doing so. First, though, there is one fundamental skill that we must develop or strengthen: the ability to listen to the self, to grasp the signals that reach us from both within and outside.

For example, our house represents us. A leaking faucet, for example, can mean that our emotions are out of control. Appliances breaking down may symbolize a malfunction in our lives.

We should also pay attention to road accidents, large or small, that may occur: our car in fact also represents us and how we travel through life.

Likewise, it is important to pay attention to the small signals that our bodies send: for example, physical injury recurring in the same area of the body. Our masculine side—the right—or feminine side—the left (it is the opposite for left-handed people)—tell us how we are living in the world and within ourselves.

The smallest of symptoms, if listened to and interpreted correctly, can prevent the onset of bigger, more serious pathologies.

We can also learn to understand the messages of illness through courses or textbooks, from the simplest to the most complex, that specialize in interpreting the symbolism of the body.

The indispensable foundation that we need to start knowing is to stop feeling fear when there should be comprehension and understanding. Once we can accomplish this, we will have the key to a more serene and prosperous future.

The Pursuit
of Well-Being

I n the past, masses of people have moved from rural environments to cities whose populations over time have become denser and denser, leading to chaos, pollution, and thought-forms such as Egregore.

Today we are also witnessing a reversal in trend: people are choosing to return to a life in nature, attracted by its enormous tangible benefits. Let's take a closer look.

Places to Live: Man and Forest Therapy

Living in a place where the surrounding frequencies are harmonic is essential for all living beings and for the overall balance of life.

In urban metropoles, frequencies are now very different from their original equilibrium. In particular, in cities where too many people live in extreme proximity, their respective auras, with their different thoughts and vibrations, interpenetrate and interfere with each other, generating confusion, aggression, and fear. The tension is such that this occurs even in those who have an averagely balanced auric body.

It is therefore important for us to try to live in places of nature, or at least visit them as often as possible.

In Forest Therapy, trees are used to purify people who have accumulated heavy energies in their everyday lives.

The first aspect to receive the benefits are the initial auric layers as they re-compact and re-balance, as obsessive thoughts such as fear are drained and removed. This allows the heart chakra to dissolve dysfunctional thoughts and eventually transform fear into love.

Science has proven that trees produce volatile elements, known as terpenes: as we breathe, they attach themselves to the receptors of the physical body, balancing different parameters in just a few hours: blood pressure, oxygen saturation levels in the blood, the reduction of cortisol (the stress hormone), and a gradual increase in the immune system regarding NK (Natural Killer) cells that deal with pathogen agents in the physical body.

Human beings, as rural beings, carry the memories of nature with us, reactivating them in the woods and allowing them to self-balance. Embracing a tree, breathing in its scents and volatile substances, is one of the most profound remedies of auric reharmonization.

The Balance between the Two Extremes: Centrality

A balanced human being should acquire the ability to fluctuate near the very center between two emotional extremes. This mechanism is explained in the Emerald Tablet, which, according to the mythology, was written around 52,000 BC by the Egyptian divinity and teacher Toth, Hermes Trismegistus, Hermes the "thrice great."

Two extreme behaviors have an unresolved issue in common: for example, extreme anger and extreme pacifism share the theme of anger management, which is expressed openly or disguised as total peace, but always in an unresolved form.

To fix the imbalance, we need to transform it until we find a new point of equilibrium.

The first step is therefore to feel our aggression, experiencing it in depth until we reach the original problem. At that point, we can embark on a short subconscious experiential journey, trying to repress the aggression and moving ourselves to a state of extreme hypofunctionality (−4): i.e., complete, repressed calm. After a brief period of this, we will feel like imploding.

We then would move to a zone of hyperactivity (+4), looking more deeply into the subject and discovering a minor charge of anger. Shaken by this emotional tremor, we then find ourselves looking for a state of peace (−3), to then experience that condition of implosion again, sensing discomfort, and therefore shifting to +3. As the experiment continues, so our anger becomes less and less explosive, as it is found in the very middle of the elaboration. We gradually move until we feel a true—yet still contrived—state of calm. We will finally realize that balanced management and resolution of the issue can be neither extreme nor static at absolute zero; rather, it is dual, oscillating constantly. We learn therefore that centrality is not rigid, but flexible, alternating moments of peace with those of healthy aggression.

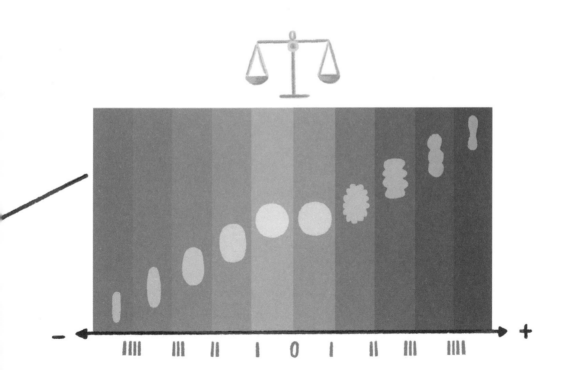

Electrosmog and the Energic System

Fvery time the vibratory speed of systems and organs changes, this affects their proper function and leads to a series of chain reactions. Some issues deriving from non-natural external origin can sometimes create really serious problems.

Several independent researchers have shown that electrosmog is one of the factors affecting human health: its frequencies change those of the body, leading to hyperfunction. The body's systems that are most at risk are the endocrine system and the immune system: for example, contact between these frequencies and the epiphysis—the gland located in the sixth chakra—inhibits the gland's correct function, producing insufficient amounts of the hormone melatonin, which helps regulate sleep and the sleep-wake cycle, consequently causing problems such as poor sleep quality and lack of attention during the day.

There are several measures you can use to mitigate the impact of these frequencies on your energy system:

+ keep mobile phones at least five feet away from the physical body, using wired headphones (not wireless or Bluetooth, which generate other harmful frequencies);

+ at night, it is good practice to keep your mobile phone in airplane mode, allowing only the main functions, such as the alarm clock and calls from favorite numbers;

+ Wi-Fi routers, which should be kept at least ten feet away from people, emit even more harmful frequencies than Wi-Fi itself—it is therefore better to use the cable connection;

+ frequencies emitted by LED lamps, especially cool white ones, are poorly tolerated by the human energy system;

+ at home, it is always good to let the air move, opening windows often and letting the house breathe.

BIBLIOGRAPHY

✦ APICELLA, LUCA, *La via della cristalloterapia, apprendere e crescere con l'autotrattamento*, Susil Edizioni

✦ APICELLA, LUCA,*The 7 Chakra Crystals: A Guide to Find Your Balance and Peace*, Andrews McMeel Publishing

✦ KAPTCHUK, TOD J., *The Web That Has No Weaver: Understanding Chinese Medicine*, McGraw Hill

✦ LEADBEATER, CHARLES WEBSTER, *Man Visible and Invisible*, Quest Books (Revised edition)

✦ OLIVIERO, FRANCESCO, *"Benattia". Significato della vita, senso della malattia e processo di autoguarigione*, Nuova Ipsa editore.

✦ O'HARE, DAVID, *Heart coherence 365: A guide to long lasting heart coherence*, Thierry Souccar Publishing

✦ POWELL, ARTHUR EDWARD, *The Mental Body*, Kessinger Pub

✦ POWELL, ARTHUR EDWARD, *Causal Body and the Ego*, Theosophical Publishing House

✦ STEINER, RUDOLPH, *An Outline of Occult Science*, Rudolf Steiner Press

Luca Apicella

Attracted by nature and the Earth's energy from a very young age, through Reiki, Luca embarked on a wonderful path that brought him closer to naturopathy and bionatural disciplines, topics that he also touches on as an author. Over the years, he has also become interested in crystal therapies and other energy disciplines, which he has learned to use as a tool for work but also a subject for teaching and sharing. In 2021, he became an expert facilitator in Forest Medicine (Shinrin-Yoku) and a psychosomatic counselor. Together with his in-person and online courses, he also holds training courses in nature and in the woods, convinced that, in the short term, a return to contact with his beloved trees and the nature from which we all come is what will make the difference.

Alessandra De Cristofaro

Alessandra works as an illustrator for magazines, communication agencies, and international publishing houses. Her work, inspired by holistic and spiritual interests, is characterized by her attention to the relationship between the inner and exterior worlds, expressed in a dreamlike, surreal dimension and elaborated in a Pop prospective.